Share it!

Workbook

6

Cheryl Pelteret

macmillan
education

Table of Contents

Welcome Unit
pages 4–7

Unit 1
We're All Different
pages 8–16

Unit 2
People We Know
pages 17–25

Share the World 1
pages 26–27

Unit 3
Around Town
pages 28–36

Unit 4
Be Creative!
pages 37–45

Share the World 2
pages 46–47

Unit 5
Awesome Experiences
pages 48–56

Unit 6
Party Time!
pages 57–65

Share the World 3
pages 66–67

Unit 7
At the Movies!
pages 68–76

Unit 8
School's Out!
pages 77–85

Share the World 4
pages 86–87

Word Work
pages 88–95

1 Complete. Use the classroom rules below.

ahead	others	~~before you speak~~

Be respectful!

Think _before you speak_ .

Be kind!

Help _____ .

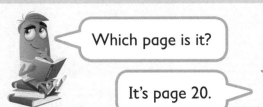

Which page is it?

It's page 20.

Be responsible!

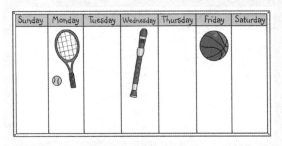

Plan _____ .

2 What other classroom rules do you know? Write two more. Then draw.

_____   _____

3 Read and write.

| Japan | Mexico | Spain | Russia | Brazil |
| the UK | China | Turkey | the USA |

1 The capital of _Spain_ is Madrid.

2 Ankara is the capital of _____ .

3 _____ has a white flag with a red circle in it.

4 The flag of _____ is green, blue, and yellow.

5 The capital of _____ is Beijing.

6 _____ is a very big country.

7 The flag of _____ is green, white. and red.

8 London is the capital of _____ .

9 The flag of _____ has red stripes and stars on it.

4 Find the continents and regions. Then complete the words.

1 A s i a

2 ___ ___ r o ___ ___ ___

3 North, South, and
Central ___ ___ ___ ___ ___ ___

4 ___ ___ ___ a ___ ___ ___ c ___

5 ___ fr ___ ___ ___

6 ___ ___ ___ ___ ___ al ___ ___

a	m	t	c	s	r	o	i	a	a
f	i	l	c	a	r	r	o	o	u
r	c	e	u	r	o	p	e	i	s
i	p	a	s	r	t	m	c	a	t
c	r	n	e	t	u	a	e	p	r
a	n	t	a	r	c	t	i	c	a
i	a	a	s	e	f	i	r	r	l
c	c	u	i	a	a	i	s	i	i
a	t	i	a	m	e	r	i	c	a
u	i	n	r	t	t	c	a	u	l

Nationalities and Languages

5 Complete with the nationalities.

1 I'm Cesar. I'm from Brazil. I'm _Brazilian_ .

2 I'm Emir. I'm from Turkey. I'm _____ .

9 I'm Harry. I'm from the UK. I'm _____ .

3 I'm Matt. I'm from Australia. I'm _____ .

8 I'm Carmen. I'm from Spain. I'm _____ .

4 I'm Adriana. I'm from Mexico. I'm _____ .

7 I'm Li. I'm from China. I'm _____ .

5 I'm Isamu. I'm from Japan. I'm _____ .

6 I'm Katie. I'm from the USA. I'm _____ .

6 Write their languages.

1 Harry, Matt, and Katie speak _English_ .

2 Emir speaks _____ .

3 Adriana and Carmen speak _____ .

4 Cesar speaks _____ .

5 Isamu speaks _____ .

6 Li speaks _____ .

7 Read and complete. Use *will* and the words below.

| be   cycle   fly   travel |

Mars is 54·6 million km from Earth.

1 In five years, my big brother ____will____

____be____ a pilot! He _____ _____

planes from the UK to Australia.

Sydney, Australia, is about 17,000 km from London, UK.

2 In the future, I _____ _____
to Mars!

The Tour de France is about 3,500 km.

3 In the future, we _____ _____ in
the Tour de France, the international
cycling race!

8 Complete the questions. Then look at the pictures in Activity 7 again and write the answers.

1 How far _____ __is__ _____ it from Earth to Mars?

_____

2 How _____ from London, UK, to Sydney, Australia?

_____

3 _____ from the start to the end of the Tour de France?

_____

Lesson 1 Vocabulary

1 Read and match.

1   I have curly hair. | f | 2   I have straight hair. | |

3   I am bald. | | 4   I have bangs. | |

5   I have big eyebrows. | | 6   I have a mustache. | |

7   I have a beard. | | 8   I have wavy hair. | |

2 Use the words in Activity 1 to write about ...

1   your teacher

   My teacher has curly hair and bangs.

2   your friend

   _____

3   somebody in your family

   _____

4   you

   _____

Student Book page 10

1 Look and complete the questions. Use *do* or *does* and *look like*.

Grandpa

My sister

Tina and Lori

1 What _____ *does* _____ your grandpa _____ *look like* _____ ?

2 What _____ your sister _____ ?

3 What _____ Tina and Lori _____ ?

My uncle

Nathan   Damian

4 What _____ your uncle _____ ?

5 What _____ Nathan and Damian _____ ?

2 Answer the questions in Activity 1. Use the words below.

| bangs   beard   curly hair   looks like   ~~mustache~~   straight hair |

1 He's bald, and he _____ *has a mustache* _____ .

2 She _____ .

3 They _____ and _____ .

4 He _____ .

5 Nathan _____ his brother Damian.

Lesson 3 Reading

1 Read Sammy's text and look at her avatar. Check (✔) the correct answers.

Sammy

Hi, Amy! I went on a great website called Avatar Me.

I made a new avatar! It's really fun. 😃

Look at my avatar. What do you think? Do you like it?

You can make one, too! 🙂

Are you ...?

a boy ☐   a girl ✔

What do you look like?

I have **big** ☐ **small** ☐ eyes.

I have **long** ☐ **short** ☐ hair.

I have **curly** ☐ **wavy** ☐ **straight** ☐ hair.

I have **black** ☐ **blond** ☐ hair.

I have **small** ☐ **big** ☐ eyebrows.

I have **glasses** ☐ .

I have a **beard** ☐ a **mustache** ☐ .

Sammy   Sammy's Avatar

2 Read Amy's text. Circle the correct answers.

Amy

Haha, Sammy! 😃 Your avatar is so funny!

You look like a different person!

My new avatar is on the website now, too. It's really fun!

1 Amy says Sammy's avatar (is)/ **isn't** funny.

2 Amy says Sammy's avatar **looks** / **doesn't look** like Sammy.

3 Amy **makes** / **doesn't make** an avatar.

4 Amy **likes** / **doesn't like** making an avatar.

1 Look at the Writing Tip. Write the adjectives in the correct order.

1 Does your sister have blue big eyes and dark small eyebrows?

   Does your sister have big blue eyes and small dark eyebrows?

2 You have red, wavy, short hair.

   _____

3 Aunt Hattie has blond curly hair, and bangs.

   _____

> **Writing Tip!** Write adjectives in this order: 1 size or length; 2 style; 3 color.
>
> *My brother has big dark eyebrows. She has long, straight, brown hair.*

2 Look at Activity 2 on page 13 of your Student Book. Think about the person you know. Complete the chart. Write two adjectives for each heading.

Eyes	Eyebrows	Hair

3 Write your descriptive paragraph. Use the information in Activity 2 on page 13 of your Student Book and in Activity 2 above. Write the adjectives in the correct order.

Name _____

_____

_____

_____

_____

_____

Lesson 5 Vocabulary

1 Write the words in the crossword.

Across

1
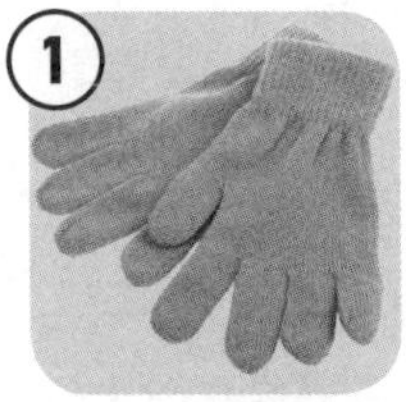
4
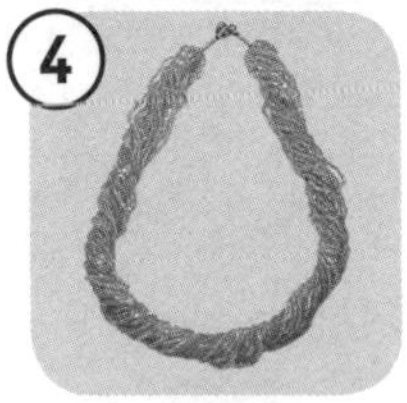
6
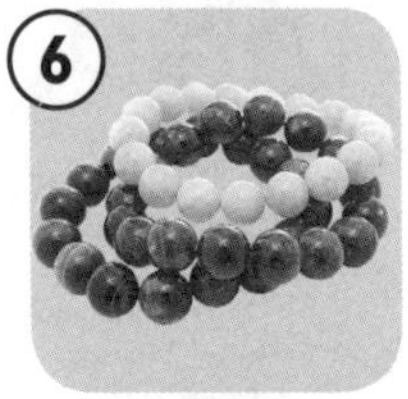
7

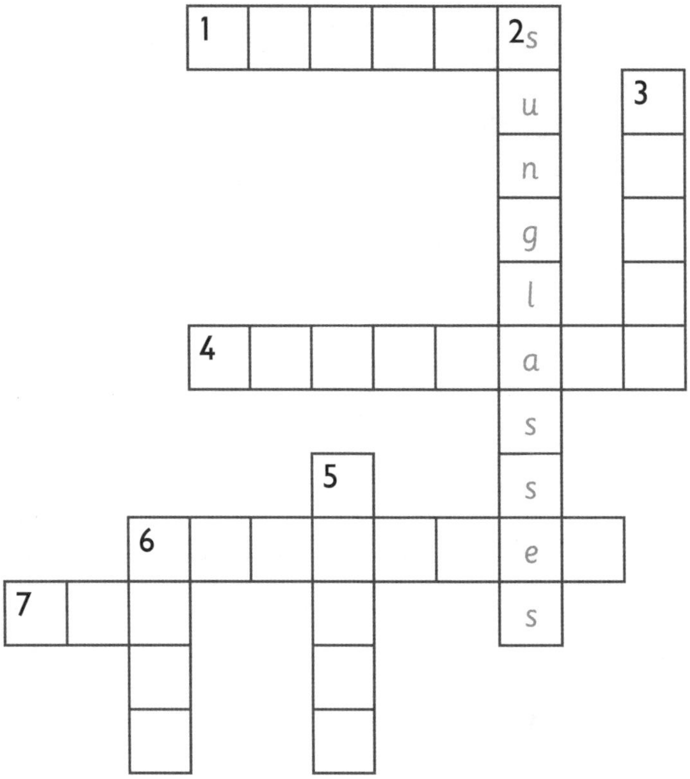

Down

2
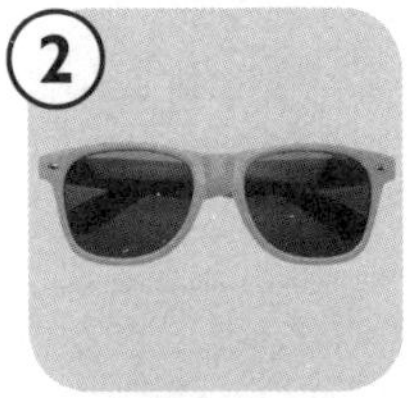
3
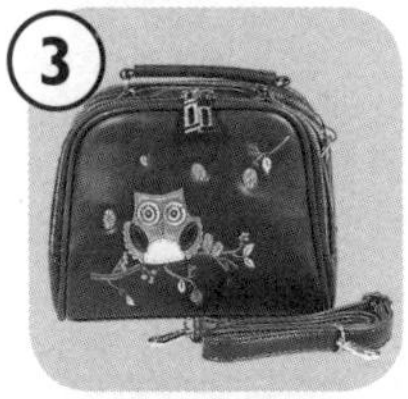
5
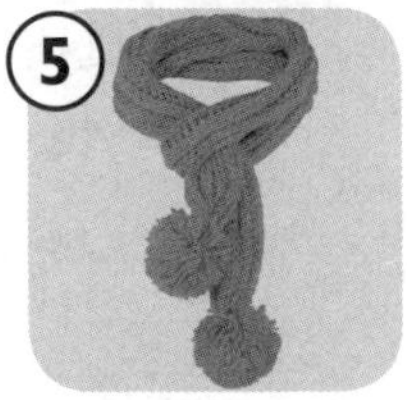
6
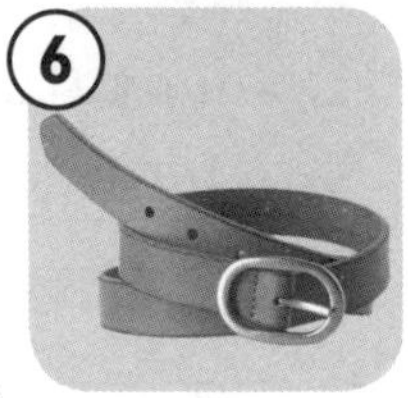

2 Complete the chart. Use six of the words in Activity 1.

1 You wear these around your neck.	2 You wear this around the middle of your body.	3 You carry this.	4 You wear this when it's sunny outside.
tie			

3 What two words are missing from Activity2? Write definitions.

1 ____________ ____

2 ____________ ____

Student Book page 14

1 Match the parts of the sentences.

1 There's the necklace

2 Milo is the boy

3 Is that the bracelet

4 My grandpa is the man

5 I can't find the purse

6 Miss Bright is the teacher

a who has a gray beard.

b that has my money and ticket in it.

c who teaches science.

d that fell off in the swimming pool!

e who sits next to me in class.

f that you got for your birthday?

2 Circle who or that.

1 A pilot is a person **who** / **that** flies a plane.

2 A tie is something **who** / **that** you wear around your neck.

3 The Browns are the people **who** / **that** live next to us.

4 Chess is a game **who** / **that** two people play together.

5 Rosie is the girl **who** / **that** painted that picture.

6 A tiger is an animal **who** / **that** lives in the jungle.

3 Complete the question. Use who or that. Then write your answer.

1 What is the subject _____that_____ you enjoy the most at school?

_____

_____

_____

1 Circle the words. Then complete.

mascellspactwinswepairsagenesgleridenticaldop

In our bodies, there are thousands of ¹ ___cells___ that carry information about what we look like. Where does this information come from? It comes from the ² _____ that we get from our parents. That is why we look like our brothers and sisters. We look like them, but we are all different. Some ³ _____ of brothers or sisters look ⁴ _____ – that means "exactly the same." These children are called ⁵ _____. Do you know any? What do they look like?

2 Write words from Activity 1.

1 This means "the same." ___identical___

2 This means "two." _____

3 You get these from your parents. _____

4 The body has thousands of these. _____

5 This means "two children born at the same time, who have the same parents." _____

3 Circle the correct words.

1 **Many people** / (**Only identical twins**) have exactly the same genes.

2 Most people in the world have **blue** / **brown** eyes.

3 The genes for **blue** / **brown** eyes are stronger than the genes for **blue** / **brown** eyes.

4 People with brown eyes **can** / **can't** have children with blue eyes.

Student Book pages 16–17

1 Complete the sentences.

| unhappy | ~~uses~~ | happy | reuses |

1

The boy _____uses_____ the bottle.

2

The girl _____ the bottle.

3

The girl is very _____!

4

The boy is _____.

2 Complete the chart.

Prefix + Word =	New Word	Sentences
un + cooked =	1 _____uncooked_____	1a He likes <u>cooked</u> meat. 1b He doesn't like <u>uncooked</u> fish.
un + tie =	2 _____	2a I can _____ my shoes. 2b I can _____ my boots.
re + write =	3 _____	3a She _____ a story. 3b She _____ the message.
re + read =	4 _____	4a I _____ a book. 4b I _____ the email.

Progress Tracker

1 Match the words and definitions.

1 It keeps your neck warm. __j__

2 You wear it around the middle of your body. ____

3 It's jewelry that you wear around your neck. ____

4 You wear them on your hands. ____

5 It's jewelry that you wear on your arm. ____

6 Hair that isn't wavy or curly is ____.

7 Some men grow a ____ or a ____ on their face.

8 Everyone has two of these above their eyes. ____

9 People who don't have hair are ____.

10 Some men wear it when they go to work. ____

a bald

b straight

c necklace

d bracelet

e tie

f eyebrows

g gloves

h belt

i beard

j scarf

k mustache

2 Track it! Rate your progress in Unit 1.

I can name words to describe appearance. ☆☆☆☆☆

I can talk about people's appearance. ☆☆☆☆☆

I can read and understand a questionnaire about appearance. ☆☆☆☆☆

I can write a descriptive paragraph. ☆☆☆☆☆

I can name fashion accessories. ☆☆☆☆☆

I can join two sentences using *who* and *that*. ☆☆☆☆☆

I can read and understand a scientific text. ☆☆☆☆☆

I can make a family tree and talk about the way I look. ☆☆☆☆☆

I can read and say words with the prefixes *un-* and *re-*. ☆☆☆☆☆

Lesson 1 Vocabulary

1 Find and circle seven words. Then complete the sentences.

z	o	s	a	d	z	b	a	o	g	c
d	i	m	f	k	t	u	t	s	w	j
q	g	a	w	l	y	p	h	j	q	i
v	f	r	i	e	n	d	l	y	s	m
p	a	t	i	e	n	t	e	w	d	p
s	k	w	r	o	i	c	t	u	f	q
t	i	y	p	c	f	n	i	h	u	u
k	n	j	o	q	b	o	c	k	n	i
l	d	c	g	x	v	p	x	f	n	e
c	o	n	f	i	d	e	n	t	y	t

1 We laugh at Lucia's stories! She's so ___funny___ !

2 Suzie talks in front of her classmates. She's very _____ .

3 Harry always gets 100% in his school work. He's a _____ boy!

4 Omar likes to help people. He's very _____ .

5 Jessica loves sports, and she's very good at them. She's very _____ .

6 Cody doesn't talk a lot. He's a _____ boy.

7 Miss Carter always takes time to help us understand things. She's a very _____ teacher.

8 Nuria talks to everyone. She always smiles and says *Hello*. She's a very _____ girl.

2 Answer the questions. Write words from Activity 1.

1 What are you like? _____

2 What's your friend like? _____

3 What's your teacher like? _____

Lesson 2 Grammar

1 Complete the questions.

Luke: Hi, Lily! What are your plans for this weekend?

Lily: I'm having lunch with my family! My cousins are coming from Canada.

Luke: What ¹ <u>are they like</u> ?

Lily: They're smart and funny!

Luke: And your aunt? What ² _____?

Lily: She's quiet and patient.

Luke: What ³ _____ your uncle

⁴ _____?

Lily: He's a P.E. teacher, so he's very athletic.

Luke: ⁵ _____ your parents

⁶ _____?

Lily: My parents are friendly and kind. Can I ask you a question?

⁷ _____? Am I like anyone in my family?

Luke: You? Yes, Lily, you're funny, kind, friendly, and smart! You *are* like them!

2 Write the questions. Add *'s* or *are*. Then write answers.

1 your / like / What / mom / ?

<u>What's your mom like?</u>

_____

2 grandparents / ? / like / What / your

_____

_____

3 like / your / ? / What / teacher

_____

_____

4 your / like / What / ? / friends

_____

_____

5 ? / you / like / What

_____

_____

Student Book page 21

1 Read. Then match the name to the adjective.

1 quiet _Elise_   2 athletic _____   3 funny _____   4 kind _____

Pen Pal World

Beatrice

I'm Beatrice. Most people call me Bea! One day, I want to be a nurse. I love helping people. I help my mom with my sisters and our pets. I also help with chores at home.

Karim

My name is Karim. I like reading comics and jokes. I also like watching comedy shows on TV! My favorite subject at school is drama. But my teachers always tell me, "Stop laughing, Karim!, and listen!" 😃

Carlos

Hello! My name is Carlos. I'm ten years old. My favorite subject is P.E. I love sports! In the summer I go swimming, and in the winter I play basketball. I go running on weekends, too!

Elise

Hello, everyone. I'm Elise. I have blond hair and glasses. I don't talk a lot, but I like writing emails and letters. That's why I want to have a pen pal. I love writing, reading, and drawing.

2 Read and answer.

1 What job does Beatrice want to do one day?

She wants to be a nurse.

2 What does Karim's drama teacher tell him?

_____

3 What does Carlos do on Saturdays and Sundays?

_____

4 Why does Elise want a pen pal?

_____

Lesson 4 Writing

1 Look at the Writing Tip. Circle the correct word.

1   Jose is friendly. He is **as well** / **also** very funny.

2   I can speak English, and I can speak a little Spanish, **also** / **too**.

3   My favorite subject is science, but I like math **as well** / **also**.

> **Writing Tip!** We use *also*, *too*, and *as well* to add more information to a sentence.
>
> *I like swimming. I **also** like playing basketball.*
>
> *I am quiet and kind. I am very patient, **too**.*
>
> *I enjoy reading, and I like listening to music **as well**.*

2 Look at Activity 2 on page 23 of your Student Book. Complete the sentences about what you are like and what you like doing.

I am _____. I am also _____.

I like _____ and I like _____ as well.

3 Write your personal profile. Use the information in Activity 2 on page 23 of your Student Book and the information above. Use *also*, *too*, and *as well*.

Student Book page 23

1 Write the adverb and complete the sentence. Use the adjective in parenthesis. Then match.

1 Look ___carefully___ before you cross the road. (careful)

2 Jack kicked the ball _____. (bad)

3 Last week, Mia did very _____ in her spelling test. (good)

4 Please work _____ in the library. (quiet)

5 She is singing _____. (loud)

6 Janine finished the race _____. (quick)

7 Be careful. Drive _____. (slow)

8 Wait _____ for somebody to answer the phone. (patient)

 (a)

 (b)

 (c)

 (d)

 (e) 1

 (f)

 (g)

 (h)

2 Complete the sentences. Use the words below.

| well | loudly | quickly | carefully |

1 My sister runs very _____!

2 I always do _____ at school.

3 Always ride your bicycle _____.

4 Don't talk _____ in class.

Lesson 6 Grammar

1 Read and complete the questions. Then write short answers.

School Activities Day!

Are you good at ...		
	Yes	No
team games?	Alys, Jack	Dee
playing a musical instrument?	Tyler, Dee	Jack
telling funny stories?	Rory, Dee	Alys, Tyler

1   _____Are_____ you good at team games, Jack? _____Yes_____ , I _____am_____ .

2   _____ you good at team games, Dee? _____ , I _____ .

3   What about Alys? _____ she good at team games? _____ ,
she _____ .

4   _____ Jack good at playing a musical instrument? _____ ,
he _____ .

5   _____ Tyler and Dee good at playing a musical instrument? _____ ,
they _____ .

6   _____ you good at telling funny stories, Alys and Tyler? _____ ,
we _____ .

2 Write complete questions. Use *Is / Are* and *good at*. Then write short answers.

1   your parents / speaking English

Are your parents good at speaking English?   Yes, they are.

2   you / singing

_____

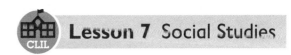

1 Complete the crossword.

Across

3 My ... is Florence Nightingale, who was a famous nurse.

4 Stories about great people ... other people.

6 My ... is to be a firefighter and save lives.

Down

1 You have to be very ... to be an astronaut.

2 Amelia Earhart is a woman who flew across the Atlantic Ocean ...

5 My ... model is my mom. She is kind and patient.

2 Read the text on page 26 of your Student Book again. Circle the correct answers.

1 Role models **can** / **can't** be people we don't know.

2 Amelia Earhart flew **across the Atlantic Ocean** / **around the world** alone.

3 The writer had an accident **on a bike** / **on a plane**.

4 It **took** / **didn't take** a long time for the paramedics to come.

5 Paramedics have to be **quiet** / **confident**.

6 The writer's dad plays the guitar **well** / **badly**.

3 Answer the question.

1 Who is your role model, and what is he / she like?

_____

1 Look and complete the sentences. Use *-ful-* or *-ly.*

1

pain _f_ _u_ _l_

2

friend____ ____

3

harm____ ____ ____

4

cost____ ____

2 Complete the chart.

Word + Suffix =	New Word	Sentences
care + ful =	1 _careful_	She's a ____careful____ driver.
color + ful =	2 _____	That's a _____ picture!
hope + ful =	3 _____	I'm very _____ about my test.
year + ly =	4 _____	We all enjoy our _____ party.
like + ly =	5 _____	They're _____ to arrive today.
nice + ly =	6 _____	You did that very _____, Bess.

1 Complete the sentences. Use the words below.

funny   patient   well   ~~quietly~~   confident   smart   carefully   kind   slowly   athletic

1   It's the opposite of loudly.   _quietly_

2   _____ people are good at sports.

3   _____ people do well at school.

4   _____ people like to help others.

5   _____ people don't get angry quickly.

6   A _____ joke makes you laugh.

7   It's the opposite of quickly. _____

8   It's the opposite of badly. _____

9   It means "to do something with care." _____

10   _____ people don't feel nervous before an exam.

2 Track it! Rate your progress in Unit 2.

I can name words to describe personality.   ☆ ☆ ☆ ☆ ☆

I can talk about people's personalities.   ☆ ☆ ☆ ☆ ☆

I can read and understand a personal profile.   ☆ ☆ ☆ ☆ ☆

I can write a personal profile.   ☆ ☆ ☆ ☆ ☆

I can name words to describe how people do things.   ☆ ☆ ☆ ☆ ☆

I can talk about what people are good at.   ☆ ☆ ☆ ☆ ☆

I can read and understand a text about role models.   ☆ ☆ ☆ ☆ ☆

I can talk about role models and why they're important.   ☆ ☆ ☆ ☆ ☆

I can read and say words with the suffixes -ful and -ly.   ☆ ☆ ☆ ☆ ☆

1 Look at the fairy tale on page 30 of your **Student Book** again. What is the message of the fairy tale? Circle the correct answer.

1 Anyone can marry a queen.

2 It's more important to be a good, kind person than a beautiful person.

3 You should always try to find someone handsome or beautiful to marry.

2 Match. Choose two endings a–h for each sentence.

1 The queen ___c___

2 The hairdresser _____ _____

3 Many men _____ _____

4 The shepherd boy _____ _____

a came to the shop in beautiful clothes.

b didn't want to look in the mirror.

c wanted to get married.

d had a useful object.

e looked after sheep.

f visited the palace.

g was sad.

h didn't feel scared to look in the mirror.

Student Book pages 30–31

3 Make a mind map of the things you often find in a fairy tale. Use the words below.

> ~~a castle~~   ~~a king~~   a hill   ~~a letter~~   rich and poor people
> a ring   a garden   a shepherd   a mirror   a queen

Fairy Tales

Places	**People**	**Things**
a castle	a king	a letter

4 Choose five words from Activity 3 above to make your own fairy tale. Then write a paragraph from your fairy tale.

_____

_____

_____

_____

5 Think of a famous fairy tale you know. What is the message of the fairy tale? How can we use this message in our lives today?

_____

_____

③ Around Town

Lesson 1 Vocabulary

1 Find and circle seven words.

1 A police officer works here.

2 You can watch sports here.

3 You can mail a letter here.

4 You can put your money here.

5 A firefighter works here.

6 You can learn about very old things here.

7 You can see a show here.

8 You can buy bread here.

p	o	l	i	c	e	s	t	a	t	i	o	n
e	s	l	c	k	u	f	v	e	p	d	p	t
f	t	e	p	h	s	r	g	t	o	o	f	b
d	a	u	d	u	n	x	h	w	s	w	g	a
m	d	s	v	i	m	z	j	q	t	x	h	n
f	i	r	e	s	t	a	t	i	o	n	l	k
e	u	s	z	d	f	b	k	s	f	c	n	h
l	m	u	s	e	u	m	l	v	f	z	b	g
z	y	l	s	z	x	w	z	b	i	q	c	l
t	h	e	a	t	e	r	y	n	c	r	e	i
e	l	q	t	a	b	d	e	s	e	f	r	o
f	n	r	b	k	b	a	k	e	r	y	x	t
g	o	y	p	h	w	l	f	x	g	b	t	r
c	n	o	i	i	y	v	c	o	i	q	i	v

2 Complete. Use the words in Activity 1.

1 People perform on stage in a _____theater_____.

2 When I need money, I go to the _____.

3 I'm going to the _____ to buy a stamp for my letter.

4 My favorite baseball team is playing at the _____ on Saturday!

5 My dad makes great cakes! He works in a _____.

6 The police officer's car is outside the _____ where he works.

7 A _____ has a lot of very old things.

8 There's a fire! Call the _____, quickly!

28

1 Look at the map and choose the correct words.

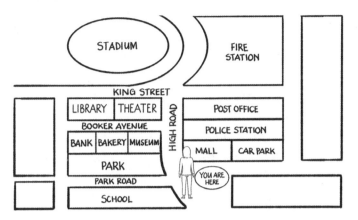

1 Where's the theater?   It's on the **(left)** / **right**, next to the library.

2 Where's the **school** / **museum**?   It's in the center of the town.

3 Where's the **fire station** / **police station**?   It's between the post office and the mall.

4 Where's the **bank** / **bakery**?   It's next to the museum.

5 Where's the post office?   It's on the corner of **King Street** / **Booker Avenue** and High Road.

2 Look again and complete.

~~across from~~   between   corner   left   next to   right

1 Where's the park?

It's _____ across from _____ the school, in Park Road.

2 Where's the car park?

It's on the _____, next to the mall.

3 Where's the theater?

It's on the _____ of King Street and High Road,

_____ the library.

4 Where's the bakery?

It's _____ the bank and the museum.

5 Where's the museum?

It's on the _____, next to the bakery.

1 Read the brochure. Write the headings in the correct places (a–c).

Other important places   What to do   Where to eat

Buxton – there's something for everyone here!

Are you thinking of coming on vacation to Buxton? You'll find something for everyone here!

Buxton has a long, interesting history. Many years ago, it was a big farm! The farmer, Jackson Greene, built a school for his workers. The school is still there – at the end of Greene Road, next to the library.

a _____

To learn more about the history of Buxton, visit the museum on High Street. It's across from the pharmacy, between the café and the bookshop.

The beautiful, modern theater is also on Bell Street, next to the park.

Go shopping in the Buxton shopping mall. Walk past the post office to the end of High Street, and the mall is opposite the park. There are a lot of different shops.

b _____

When you are hungry, go to the bakery on the corner of Bell Street and High Street. It's across from the fire station. The food is very good!

c _____

Post your letters from the post office. It's across the road from the café, on the corner of High Street and Greene Road.

There is a bank on High Street, next to the post office.

Enjoy your vacation in our beautiful town!

2 Reread the brochure and look at the map. Then label.

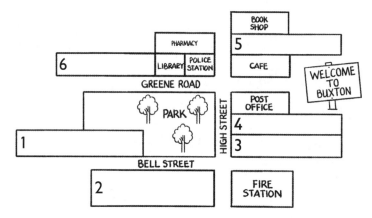

1 Look at the Writing Tip. Write the capital letters.

1 Our town, seaview, has the best pizza restaurant in the world! It's just across from queen's park. It's called mario's pizza place.

2 At the corner of park street and hill avenue, there's a great candy store called candymania.

> **Writing Tip!** Use capital letters for the names of streets, towns, places in a town, and buildings.
>
> *I'm a student at Ashton High School.*
>
> *It's on Mill Street.*
>
> *The Tate Gallery of Modern Art is in London.*
>
> *There is a big festival in Hyde Park.*

2 Write your travel brochure. Use the information in Activity 2 on page 37 of your Student Book. Write the name of your place. Use capital letters in the correct places.

Welcome to _____ !

_____

_____

_____

_____

_____

_____

_____

_____

_____

1 Match the pictures and the directions.

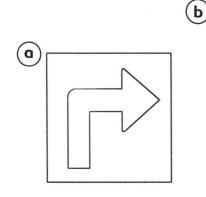
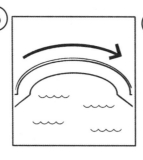
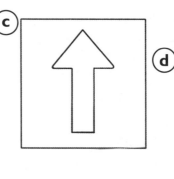
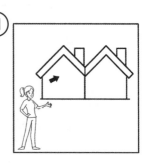

1 Go straight.	c	2 Turn around and go back.	___
3 Go past the library.	___	4 Turn right.	___
5 It's on the left.	___	6 Walk across the road.	___
7 Walk along the river.	___	8 Go over the bridge.	___

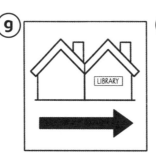
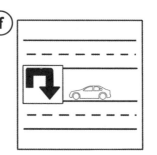
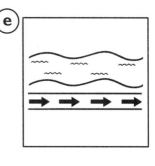

2 Complete. Use the words below.

across   g̶o̶   on   over   past   turn

Here's how to get to the theater from the train station. ¹_____Go_____ straight along

Station Road and ²_____ left at the corner. Walk ³_____ the street to the

other side. Go straight along the road, ⁴_____ the mall. You come to a small bridge.

Go ⁵_____ the bridge. You can see the theater in front of you. It's ⁶_____ the

right, next to the bookstore.

Student Book page 38

1 Look at the map. Order the words and write the directions.

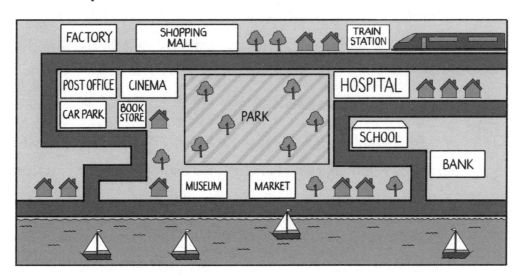

1 I'm at the museum. The sea is in front of me. How do I get to the bank?
First, / Then / turn left, and it's on the right / turn left, and walk past the market / .

First, turn left and walk past the market. Then turn left, and it's on the right.

2 I'm at the school. I can see the park at the end of the street. How do I get to the hospital?
walk along the side of the park / turn right / Then / First, / .

3 I'm inside the bookstore. How do I get to the sea?
Then / First, / follow the road until you get to the sea / come out of the bookstore, and turn left / .

4 I'm standing outside the post office. I'm across from the factory. How do I get to the train station?
walk past the shopping mall, / It's opposite / the hospital / First, / cross the road / Then / .

Lesson 7 Social Studies

1 Circle the words. Then complete.

becauseyoucan'tscalealways**compass**usegridyourdistancephonekeyorsymbolstablet

We all need maps to help us to find where to go. The 1 _compass_ in the corner

shows us which way is north, south, east, or west. Maps also have small pictures, called

2 _____. They tell us what different places are, for example, a road or a river.

The 3 _____ shows us what the small pictures are. Maps also have squares with

numbers on them. This is a 4 _____, and it helps us to find places. The

5 _____ on a map shows us the 6 _____ between different places.

2 Use the extra words in the word snake to answer the question: Why is it important to learn to read a paper map?

_____

3 Label the pictures. Use four words from Activity 1.

1
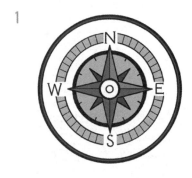

_____

2

_____

3

_____ and _____

1 **Look and complete with compound words. Join the words below.**

| pop   bed   jelly   corn   fish   room |

1

My _____ is great!

2

I like _____.

3

_____ live in the sea.

2 **Complete the chart.**

Word + Word =	New Word	Sentences
birth + day =	1 *birthday*	It's my ___*birthday*___ today!
hair + brush =	2 _____	I have a blue _____.
rain + bow =	3 _____	A _____ has a lot of colors.
bath + tub =	4 _____	We have a big _____ in the bathroom.

Progress Tracker

1 **Match the words and definitions.**

> turn   around   ~~fire station~~   over   bakery   theater
> across   bank   straight   stadium

1 A firefighter works at a _fire station_.

2 You can buy bread at a _____.

3 You can walk _____ a bridge.

4 Go _____ along this road.

5 You can put money in the _____.

6 _____ right when you get to the museum.

7 You can watch sports at a _____.

8 You can go to a show at the _____.

9 The hospital is _____ from the police station.

10 When you get to the end of the road, turn _____ and come back again.

2 **Track it!** **Rate your progress in Unit 3.**

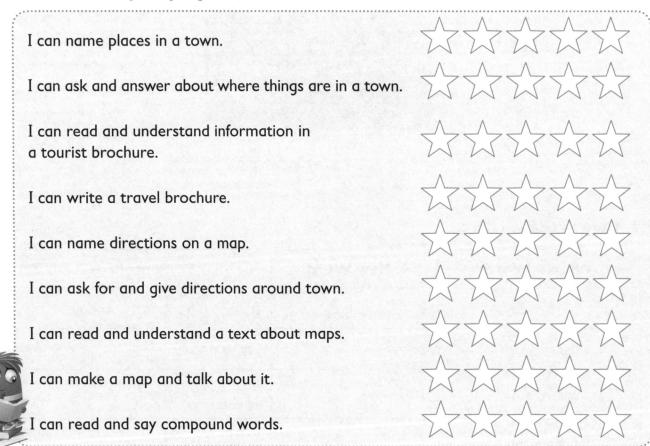

I can name places in a town.

I can ask and answer about where things are in a town.

I can read and understand information in a tourist brochure.

I can write a travel brochure.

I can name directions on a map.

I can ask for and give directions around town.

I can read and understand a text about maps.

I can make a map and talk about it.

I can read and say compound words.

Lesson 1 Vocabulary

1 Find and circle. Then label.

1

leather

2

_____

3

_____

4

_____

l	e	a	t	h	e	r
c	p	a	p	e	r	c
l	u	z	w	g	c	l
o	t	w	o	o	l	a
t	v	g	n	l	d	y
h	w	o	o	d	d	u
p	l	a	s	t	i	c

5

_____

6
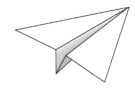
_____

7

_____

8

_____

2 Answer the questions. Write words from Activity 1.

1 What are your shoes made of? _____

2 What is your book made of? _____

3 What is your T-shirt made of? _____

1 Look and complete.

1

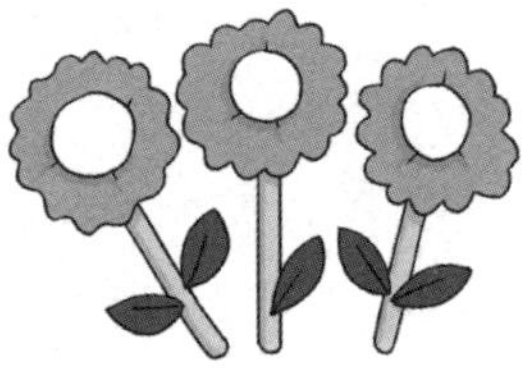

What _____are they made of_____ ?

_____They're made of_____ paper.

2

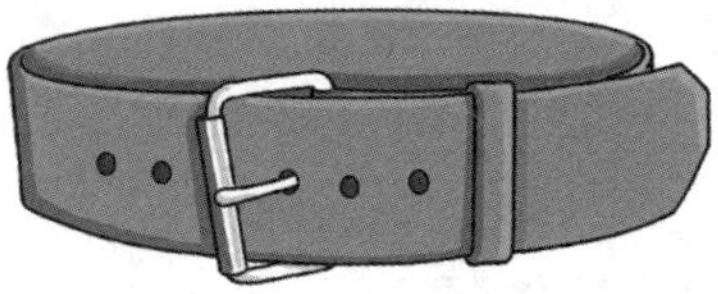

What _____ ?

_____ leather.

3

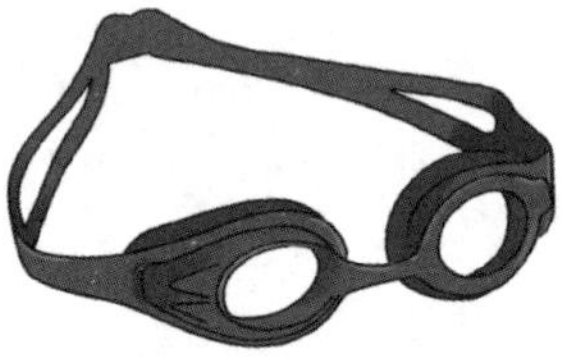

What _____ ?

_____ plastic.

4

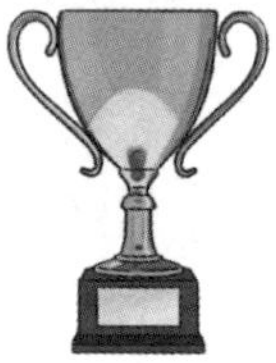

What _____ ?

_____ gold.

5

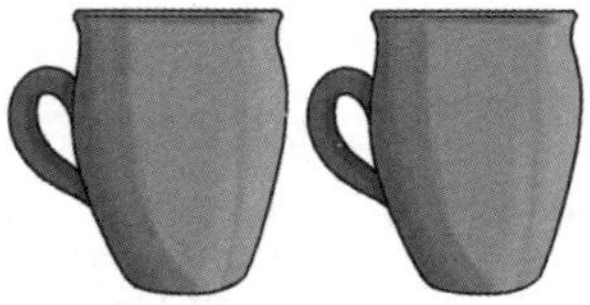

What _____ ?

_____ clay.

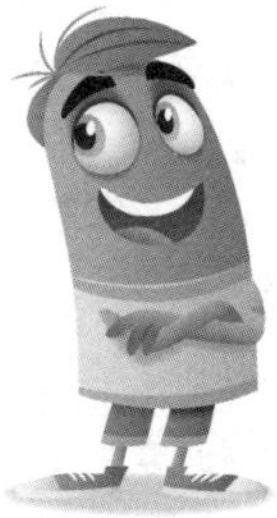

2 Write questions and answers.

1 Think of two things that are made of the same material.

What _are_ _____ ?

_____

2 Think of one thing from your school bag or pencil case.

What _____ ?

_____

1 **Read about what Nisha makes. Number the objects in the order they appear in the text.**

Meet the Artist!

Reporter: Today, we are talking to a young artist named Nisha Daley. Nisha, you make a lot of different things, using different materials. What inspires you?

Nisha: I live by the sea, and that inspires me! I find things when I walk on the beach, or I see things that give me ideas. For example, this picture is made of small pieces of sea glass. I found them on the beach, too. I used glue and an old table mat, and I made this glass picture of a fish.

Reporter: It's beautiful. What about this? Is it a ball? What's it made of?

Nisha: It's made of wool. I think it looks like a sea animal I saw on the beach! The sea animal was brown, but I made it in red. It's for my hat!

Reporter: Do you make things from clay, too?

Nisha: Yes, I do. We use clay in our art lessons. I made this bowl. I use it on my desk.

Reporter: It's very good! The flower pot is great, too! What's it made of?

Nisha: It's made of plastic. I used an old plastic bottle. I cut the bottle in half and painted it pink.

Reporter: What a smart idea! I like this, too. Is it a bird?

Nisha: Yes. It's made of paper. It's origami, from Japan. I'm not very good at it, but I practice a lot! Right now, I'm making an origami star out of gold paper.

Reporter: It's awesome! Thanks for showing us your work, Nisha!

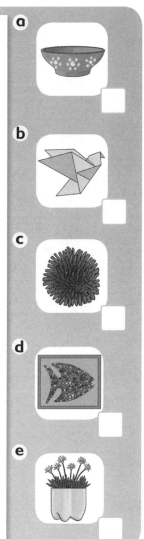

a
b
c
d
e

2 **Read again. Check (✔) the correct sentences.**

1 She used wool to make a ball for her hat. ✔

2 Nisha made a picture from plastic she found on the beach. ☐

3 The flower pot is made of clay. ☐

4 Nisha made a bowl at school. ☐

5 Nisha is good at origami. ☐

6 Right now, she is making something out of gold. ☐

Lesson 4 Writing

1 **Look at the Writing Tip. Choose A / An and write the adjectives in the correct order.**

1   A / An – leather / brown / long / expensive – belt

_____

2   A / An – red / soft / wool / new – scarf

_____

Writing Tip! We write adjectives in the following order when we are describing something.

Opinion	Size	Age	Shape	Color	Material	–
A beautiful	big	old	round	blue	clay	pot
–	A small	new	–	red	plastic	toy

2 **Write your descriptive paragraph. Use the information in Activity 2 on page 47 of your Student Book. Remember to write the adjectives in the correct order.**

1 Complete the crossword.

Across

2 The opposite of cheap.

3 The opposite of soft.

4 A lemon tastes …

5 Strawberries are …

Down

1 Something that tastes nice is …

3 Something that isn't nice.

1 d
e
l
i
c
i
o
u
s

2

3

4

5

2 Circle the correct words.

1 Sugar tastes **sweet** / **sour**.

2 I don't like this cheese. It's **delicious** / **horrible**.

3 The queen's necklace is very **cheap** / **expensive**.

4 I broke my tooth on this candy, because it was so **soft** / **hard**.

5 Urgh! This lemon is very **delicious** / **sour**.

6 Yum! I love chocolate cake. It's **delicious** / **horrible**!

7 This jelly is delicious – sweet and **hard** / **soft**.

Lesson 6 Grammar

1 Complete the questions and write the answers.

1

What _____does it smell like_____ ? (smell)

_____It smells like_____ flowers.

2

What _____? (taste)

_____ strawberries.

3

What _____? (feel)

_____ so soft!

4

What _____? (smell)

_____ delicious.

5

What _____? (feel)

_____ round, like a ball!

6

What _____? (taste)

_____ horrible.

2 Write complete questions and answers. Use the words in parentheses.

1 What _____does this fruit juice smell like_____? (this fruit juice / smell)

_____It smells like oranges._____ (oranges)

2 What _____? (this sweater / feel)

_____ (soft)

3 What _____? (chocolates / taste)

_____ (sweet)

Student Book page 49

1 Complete.

cool   dry   natural materials   straw   ~~traditional~~   wet

This is a cob house. It isn't a modern house; it's a very

1 _____traditional_____ way of building houses. Cob houses are easy and cheap to build because they only use

2 _____, for example, clay, water, sand, and 3 _____.

Clay is a good building material, because when you mix it with water, it becomes 4 _____, and you can form different shapes with it. Then, in the sun, the clay becomes

5 _____ and hard, and this makes cob houses very strong. Cob houses are very popular in hot countries, because they are 6 _____ inside.

2 Answer the questions.

1 What are two reasons why cob houses are popular?

_____

2 What are two things that you can find on the roof of a cob house?

_____

3 What are two places where you can find material for doors on a cob house?

_____

1 Look and complete the sentences. Use *-er* or *-est*.

1

This cat runs fast_e___r_ than that cat.

2

The black dog runs the slow____ ____ ____.

3

The girl is short____ ____ than the boy.

4

The boy is the short____ ____ ____.

2 Complete the chart.

Word + Suffix =	New Word	Sentences
big + er =	1 bigger	He's ___bigger___ than his friend.
tall + er =	2 _____	She's _____ than her sister.
slow + est =	3 _____	The white dog is the _____.
fat + est =	4 _____	The old cat is the _____.

44

1 Complete the sentences. Use the words below.

| clay | cloth | delicious | gold | horrible | ~~paper~~ | plastic | soft | sweet | wool |

1 The pages of a book are made of _____paper_____.

2 Cob houses are made of straw and _____.

3 Very expensive jewelry can be made of _____.

4 Urgh! Sour lemons taste _____.

5 _____ foods, for example, ice cream and candy, aren't good for your teeth, but

I love them! I think they taste _____!

6 To help the environment, we should use paper or _____ bags, not

_____ bags.

7 A scarf made of _____ keeps you warm. It also feels nice and _____.

2 Track it! Rate your progress in Unit 4.

I can name materials. ☆☆☆☆☆

I can talk about what things are made of. ☆☆☆☆☆

I can read and understand a leaflet for a festival. ☆☆☆☆☆

I can write a descriptive paragraph. ☆☆☆☆☆

I can name more describing words. ☆☆☆☆☆

I can talk about what things feel, smell, and taste like. ☆☆☆☆☆

I can read and understand a text about unusual buildings. ☆☆☆☆☆

I can talk about houses that are made of natural materials. ☆☆☆☆☆

I can read and say comparative and superlative words. ☆☆☆☆☆

1 Why did the writer write the article? Circle the correct answer.

1 To encourage tourists to visit Harbin in winter.

2 To describe daily life for people who live in Harbin.

3 To give us directions to different places in Harbin.

2 Which of the following information is <u>not</u> in the article? Check (✔).

1 How old the festival is ☐

2 Different kinds of ice and snow sculptures you can see at the festival ☐

3 Some of the famous ice artists whose work you can see at the festival ☐

4 What happens at night ☐

5 The weather ☐

6 Different places you can stay while you are in Harbin ☐

7 What you should wear ☐

8 Things to see, do, and buy ☐

Student Book pages 54–55

3 Complete the poster.

The Harbin International Ice and Snow Sculpture Festival

1 Country: _____

2 Months: _____ and _____

3 Date the festival started: _____

4 Where the ice comes from: _____

5 Where to find the theaters, museums, and stores: _____

6 Where to go shopping: _____

7 Two foods to try that taste unusual (and what they taste like):
_____, _____

4 Think. Answer the questions.

1 Do you want to visit this festival? Why or why not?

_____

_____

2 Why are national festivals important?

_____

_____

5 Write about a national festival in your country. What, where, and when is it? What can you see or do there?

_____

_____

_____

_____

Lesson 1 Vocabulary

1 Complete. Then match 1–9 to the pictures a–i.

climb   explore   go   fly   hold   meet   ride   see   sleep

1 I want to _____climb_____ to the top of a volcano.   `c`

2 Do you want to _____ on a safari in Africa?   ☐

3 She wants to _____ a snake.   ☐

4 They want to _____ a rainforest.   ☐

5 They'd like to _____ a camel one day.   ☐

6 We want to _____ in a hot air balloon.   ☐

7 She wants to _____ a famous person.   ☐

8 They _____ in the desert in tents.   ☐

9 Do you want to _____ the pyramids?   ☐

a

b

c

d

e

f

g

h

i

Student Book page 58

1 Complete the questions. Use the words in parentheses. Then write short answers.

1 Have you ever (see) _____seen_____ a snake? _____No, I haven't._____

2 Has your mom ever (make) _____ a cake? _____

3 Has your friend ever (go) _____ to London? _____

4 Have you ever (meet) _____ a famous person? _____

5 Have you ever (explore) _____ your town? _____

6 Have you ever (fly) _____ in a plane? _____

7 Have your friends ever (ride) _____ a bike? _____

8 Have you ever (sleep) _____ in a tent? _____

2 Write questions with *ever*. Then write answers.

1 you / hold / a spider? (✘)

Have you ever held a spider? No, I haven't.

2 your parents / see / a pyramid? (✘)

_____

3 your father / sleep / in the desert? (✔)

_____

4 you / fly / in a hot air balloon? (✔)

_____

5 your mother / go / on safari? (✘)

_____

6 you and your friends / climb / a volcano? (✘)

_____

1 Read. Then match the headings to paragraphs 1–3.

a Help Animals! ☐   b Climb a Volcano! ☐   c Explore a Rainforest! ☐

● ○ ○

Come to Costa Rica!

Have an experience you'll love!

Do you want to explore a rainforest?

Do you love helping animals? Have you ever climbed a volcano?

Costa Rica has something for everyone!

1   Did you know that rainforests cover 25 percent of Costa Rica? In the wonderful "cloud forest," you can walk across a high bridge between the trees. You can see beautiful birds, as well as monkeys, spiders, and frogs. You can also ride on an amazing zipline across the tops of the trees! Wear a raincoat. It's never cold, but it's often wet in the rainforest – especially in the rainy season, from May to the end of November.

2   Costa Rica is home to many species of birds, fish, and animals. It's famous for its turtles. You can help to save them at one of the country's special turtle programs. There's also an animal rescue center, where you can hold a baby sloth! Of course, Costa Rica has many snakes and spiders, too – but don't worry – you won't often meet them!

3   The fantastic Arenal volcano is in the center of Costa Rica! You can climb to the top of the volcano – or you can fly above it in a hot air balloon. Try to find a hotel with a view of the volcano. You can sometimes see smoke coming out of the top!

2 Answer the questions.

1   Why do you need a raincoat in the rainforest?   *Because it's often wet.*

2   When is the rainy season?   _____

3   Write seven different animals you can see in Costa Rica.

_____

4   What can you do on a turtle program?   _____

5   Write three ways you can see the Arenal volcano.

_____

50

1 Look at the Writing Tip. Replace the underlined words with pronouns.

1 Turtles lay ~~the turtles'~~ *their* eggs on beaches. This can be dangerous for the eggs, because some birds and animals eat <u>the eggs</u>.

2 People often book hotels where <u>people</u> can see the Arenal volcano. Sometimes, smoke comes out of the top of <u>the volcano</u>.

> **Writing Tip!** Use pronouns instead of repeating a noun in a sentence.
>
> *Jack likes to spend his vacation doing exciting things. <u>Jack</u> likes climbing volcanoes.* ✗
>
> *Jack likes to spend his vacation doing exciting things. <u>He</u> likes climbing volcanoes.* ✔
>
> *A sloth climbs trees. <u>The sloth</u> uses its three toes to climb <u>trees</u>.* ✗
>
> *A sloth climbs trees. <u>It</u> uses its three toes to climb <u>them</u>.* ✔

2 Write your advertisement. Use the information in Activity 2 on page 61 of your Student Book. Remember to use pronouns instead of repeating nouns in a sentence.

Lesson 5 Vocabulary

1 Complete the puzzle. Then write the mystery word.

1	p	o	l	a	r	b	e	a	r

Mystery word: _____

2 Answer the questions. Write words from Activity 1.

1 Which bird has a very long neck? _____

2 Which two animals are "big cats"? _____ and _____

3 Which big, heavy animal is white? _____

4 Which animal moves very slowly? _____

5 Which bird has wide wings? _____

6 Which big animal eats plants in forests and lakes? _____

7 Which animal can jump very high? _____

Student Book page 62

1 Match the parts of the sentences.

1　I've never been to Costa Rica,

2　I've never held a snake,

3　I've never tried a burger cake,

4　I've never met a famous person,

5　I've never ridden an elephant,

6　I've never climbed a volcano,

a　but I've flown above one in a hot air balloon.

b　but I've seen a lot of famous people on TV.

c　but I've eaten a burger!

d　but I've seen one in the zoo.

e　but I've been to Panama, which is next to it.

f　but I've been horseback riding.

2 Read Pablo's list and write sentences. Use *but*, *never*, and the correct form of the verbs.

Pablo: things to do before I am 11 years old!

• Ride a camel [✔], and go in a hot air balloon [✗]

• Visit a safari park [✔], and hold a snake! [✗]

• Go swimming in a lake [✔], and swim one kilometer [✗]

• Travel to New York [✗], and go to London [✔]

1　He's _____ridden_____ a camel, _____but_____ he's _____never been_____ in a hot air balloon.

2　He's _____ a safari park, _____ he's _____ a snake.

3　He's _____ swimming in a lake, _____ he's _____ one kilometer.

4　He's _____ to New York, _____ he's _____ to London.

3 Complete the sentence about you.

1　I've _____, but I've never _____

Lesson 7 Science CLIL

1 Complete.

> cut down   discover   extinct   ~~tropical~~

Many animal species live in the ¹ tropical areas of our
planet. The colorful toucan lives in the Amazon rainforest
in South America, for example. Every year, scientists
² _____ unusual and interesting species that they've
never seen before. But there's one problem. Many of these species
are endangered, because we ³ _____ their homes in the trees of the rainforests to
make paper out of the wood or to use the land for ourselves and animals. So one day, these
unusual species will all become ⁴ _____ . We need to protect the rainforests and all
the species that live there.

2 Complete the definitions. Use the words in Activity 1.

1 The opposite of "to plant" cut down

2 An area with hot, wet weather, for example, the Amazon rainforest _____

3 The same as "to find someone new" _____

4 A species that has died _____

3 Complete the sentences. Use one to three words.

1 Scientists discover new species when they _____.

2 Scientists discovered a pink _____ in a river.

3 Explorers found fire-tailed zogue zogues because there aren't so

    _____ now.

4 We use plants from the rainforest to _____.

5 To help protect the rainforests, we can _____.

1 Look and complete the sentences. Use –s, –es, –ing, or –ed.

1

They plant_____ _____ a tree yesterday.

2

Look at the small dog_____!

3

The girl is sleep _____ _____ _____

4

The box_____ _____ have a lot of

toy_____ in them.

2 Complete the chart.

Word + Ending =	New Word	Sentences
cat + s =	1 _____ *cats*	I love black and white _____ *cats* _____ !
class + es =	2 _____	English _____ are fun!
kick + ed =	3 _____	You _____ the ball hard!
paint + ing =	4 _____	They're _____ a picture.

Progress Tracker

1 Circle the correct words.

1	You can explore it.	(rainforest) / safari / hot air balloon
2	You can hold it.	moose / desert / snake
3	You can fly in it.	safari / eagle / hot air balloon
4	It's a big cat.	jaguar / kangaroo / sloth
5	It can fly.	ostrich / sloth / eagle
6	You can ride it.	hot air balloon / camel / pyramids
7	You can climb it.	desert / safari / volcano
8	Have you ever met one?	famous person / pyramids / rainforest
9	It has four legs.	eagle / moose / ostrich
10	It can jump seven meters.	polar bear / snow leopard / kangaroo

2 Track it! Rate your progress in Unit 5.

I can name awesome experiences. ☆ ☆ ☆ ☆ ☆

I can ask and answer about what I've done in the past. ☆ ☆ ☆ ☆ ☆

I can read and understand an online advertisement. ☆ ☆ ☆ ☆ ☆

I can write an advertisement. ☆ ☆ ☆ ☆ ☆

I can name animals from around the world. ☆ ☆ ☆ ☆ ☆

I can say what I've never done. ☆ ☆ ☆ ☆ ☆

I can understand a text about discovering new species. ☆ ☆ ☆ ☆ ☆

I can talk about the rainforest and why it's important. ☆ ☆ ☆ ☆ ☆

I can read and say words with –s, –es, –ing, and –ed. ☆ ☆ ☆ ☆ ☆

Student Book page 67

Lesson 1 Vocabulary

1 Circle the correct word.

Amy: Let's have a party! We can ¹ (send) / **make** invitations to all our classmates.

Leila: We need to ² **buy** / **borrow** chairs. Our neighbors have some.

Amy: Let's ³ **choose** / **decorate** the yard with balloons! And let's ⁴ **organize** / **decorate** the games.

Leila: Yes. We need to ⁵ **borrow** / **buy** the prizes. We can find them at the store.

Amy: Can I ⁶ **choose** / **make** the music? I love dancing!

Leila: Sure. And then we can ⁷ **borrow** / **prepare** the party food.

Amy: Mum can ⁸ **send** / **make** a costume.

Leila: Fantastic!

2 Match the pictures to the sentences in Activity 1. Write 1–8.

a  6

b

c

d

e

f

g

h

1 Write complete sentences.

1 yet / bought / the prizes / ? / you / Have

   Have you bought the prizes yet?

2 I've / already / Yes, / bought / them / .

   _____

3 the yard / ? / they / yet / Have / decorated

   _____

4 they / haven't decorated / yet / it / No, / .

   _____

2 Look and write. Use yet and *already*.

Party preparations!

Organize the games – Alex ✔   *Make the costumes – Olivia and Georgia ✗*

Choose the music – Mika ✔   *Prepare the party food – Bobbi and Ryan ✗*

Send invitations – Carlo ✔

1 _____Has_____ **Alex** _____ organized the games yet _____?

   Yes, he's already organized them.

2 _____ **Mika** _____?

   _____

3 _____ **Olivia and Georgia** _____?

   _____

4 _____ **Bobbi and Ryan** _____?

   _____

5 _____ **you** _____, Carlo?

   _____

Student Book page 69

1 Read Rosie's invitation and Jonah's reply. What kind of party is it?

1 A birthday party   2 A family party   3 A class party

To: jonah@homemail.com
From: rosie@housenet.com
Date: June 20
Subject: We're having a party!   SEND

Hi Jonah,

We're going to have a party for our drama club next Friday! It's at 3 o'clock, in the English classroom. We're sending an invitation to Mr. Davis, too! He's leaving the school at the end of this term, so it's also a goodbye party for him. I've organized a quiz, but I haven't bought any prizes yet.

Can you come? Please send me an email if you can come. We need to prepare the party food, so we need to know how many people are coming!

Love,

Rosie

To: rosie@housenet.com
From: jonah@homemail.com
Date: June 21
Subject: Party!   SEND

Hi Rosie,

Thanks for your invitation. Yes, I'd love to come!

I can't wait for the quiz – you know how much I love quizzes! I have some balloons to decorate the classroom.

Let's buy Mr. Davis a present. How about a CD? Do you want to come to the music store with me to choose one for him?

Love,

Jonah

2 Match the sentence halves.

1 Mr. Davis is going to

2 Rosie has already

3 Rosie hasn't

4 Rosie and her friends need to

5 Jonah loves

6 Jonah is going to help

a bought the prizes yet.

b organized a quiz.

c quizzes.

d leave the school.

e prepare food for the party.

f decorate the classroom.

Lesson 4 Writing

1 Look at the Writing Tip. Add apostrophes.

1 It's my birthday on Saturday, and Im having a party!

2 Weve borrowed some chairs from our friends houses.

3 Mr. Davis likes music. Hes got a lot of CDs.

> **Writing Tip!** We use an apostrophe:
>
> – to show possession: Kevin's football / the two boys' bikes
>
> – to show contractions: I am = I'm   he is = he's   you have = you've

2 Write your invitation email. Use the information in Activity 2 on page 71 of your Student Book. Remember to use apostrophes correctly.

To:	
From:	
Date:	
Subject:	SEND

_____

_____

_____

_____

_____

_____

_____

_____

_____

Student Book page 71

1 Complete the poster

together   the mail   water   volunteer   tutor   trash can   ~~neighborhood~~

Our Neighborhood!

Do you live in this ¹neighborhood? Do you want to help your community?

Would you like to be a ² _____? There are a lot of different things you

can do to help your neighbors. You can start by picking up litter on your streets

or on beaches. Litter should be in a ³ _____ _____!

Is your neighbor sick, or in the hospital? Why don't you ⁴ _____ the

plants, or collect ⁵ _____ _____ for them?

Are you good at English or math? Do you want to be a ⁶ _____? A lot of

children need help with their homework.

Let's all work ⁷ _____ and show that we are proud of our community!

2 Think. Write one more activity to help the neighborhood.

_____

3 Write the words from Activity 1 for the definitions.

1 To do things with other people _____work together_____

2 A person who does something without getting money for it _____

3 Work as a teacher _____

4 The area where we live _____

5 Take the letters and cards out of the mail box _____

Lesson 6 Grammar

1 Circle *for* or *since*.

1 I've lived in this house **for** / (since) I was born.

2 I've studied English **for** / **since** four years.

3 We've had this car **for** / **since** last year.

4 I haven't seen my cousin in Australia **for** / **since** we were three years old.

5 I've had the same coat **for** / **since** five years.

6 It hasn't rained a lot **for** / **since** last month.

2 Write *for* or *since*. Then write complete sentences with the correct form of the verb.

1 My dad / work / at the bank / _____ for _____ / 20 years.

My dad has worked at the bank for 20 years.

2 It / not snow / here / _____ / the last three years.

_____

3 I / know / my best friend / _____ / we were babies.

_____

4 Miss Carter / teach / us / _____ / last year.

_____

5 I / not swim / in the sea / _____ / July.

_____

6 We / not go / skateboarding / _____ / a long time.

_____

Student Book page 73

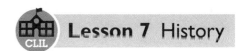

1 Complete. Use the words in the box.

~~competition~~   cartoon   exhibition
filled   model   ribbons

I'm Juan. I'm from Mexico. Every summer, there is a piñata ¹competition at our local museum. The museum shows all the piñatas in a big ² _____ , which everyone can come and see. The winner gets a prize. Last year, my piñata was a ³ _____ of a spider. I painted it black and red and decorated it with eight black ⁴ _____ for its legs. I didn't want it to look scary, so I painted a funny face on it, like a ⁵ _____ . I ⁶ _____ it with a lot of candy. I was very happy when I won a prize!

2 Read and circle *True* or *False*.

1 Traditional piñatas are made of paper.   True / (False)

2 The Chinese have had piñatas for many years.   True / False

3 At New Year in China, children threw oranges at piñatas.   True / False

4 In Spain, people made clay jars and decorated them with ribbons.   True / False

5 In Mexico, you can decorate clay jars made by artists.   True / False

6 The traditional piñata in Mexico looks like a cartoon character.   True / False

3 Design and draw a piñata.

Lesson 8 Word Study | More Prefixes (mis-, mid-, pre-, under-)

1 Complete the sentences.

| midnight | preplan | underground | ~~misnumbered~~ |

1

The girl <u>misnumbered</u> the boxes.

2

A lot of animals live _____.

3

The clock says _____.

4

I always _____ my day.

2 Complete the chart.

Prefix + Word =	New Word	Sentences
mis + read =	1 misread	You ___misread___ my notes.
pre + heat =	2 _____	I need to _____ the oven.
mid + week =	3 _____	It's Wednesday today – _____.
under + water =	4 _____	I can swim _____!

1 Match 1–10 to a–j.

1	send	*e*	a	the plants
2	borrow	___	b	the mail
3	decorate	___	c	the prizes
4	choose	___	d	the party food
5	organize	___	e	invitations
6	buy	___	f	chairs
7	prepare	___	g	together
8	collect	___	h	the yard
9	water	___	i	the games
10	work	___	j	the music

2 Track it! Rate your progress in Unit 6.

I can name party preparation activities. ☆☆☆☆☆

I can ask and answer questions using *yet* and *already*. ☆☆☆☆☆

I can read and understand an email invitation. ☆☆☆☆☆

I can write an invitation email. ☆☆☆☆☆

I can name activities to help people in the neighborhood. ☆☆☆☆☆

I can ask and answer about the past with *for* and *since*. ☆☆☆☆☆

I can read and understand a text about piñatas. ☆☆☆☆☆

I can create a design for a piñata. ☆☆☆☆☆

I can read and say words with the prefixes *mis–*, *mid–*, *pre–*, and *under–*. ☆☆☆☆☆

1 Number the sentences in the correct order.

a The boys walked around a lake. ☐

b The boys hid in the grass. ☐

c The boys packed their bags. 1

d The boys ran home. ☐

e The boys walked for two days. ☐

f The bird threw the lightning on the ground. ☐

g An enormous bird flew over them. ☐

h It started to rain. ☐

i The boys ate a meal. ☐

j The bird had something yellow in its mouth. ☐

2 Write the words in the crossword.

Across

1 When they become filled with water, it rains.

4 The loud sound you hear when there's a storm.

5 It can make things fall down, for example, trees.

Down

2 A flash of light in the sky when there's a storm.

3 The space above the Earth.

```
1      2              3
c      l   o   u   d  s


                      
                      


4


  5
```

3 Circle the correct answers.

1 The boys went to the lake because …

   a they thought that's where lightning came from.

   b they wanted to see a thunderbird.

2 They packed a bag with some …

   a warm clothes.

   b food.

3 The first thing the huge bird made was …

   a wind.

   b rain.

4 Think. Answer the question. Then draw.

Imagine you are going on an adventure for two days. What will you pack in your bag? And why?

7 At the Movies!

Lesson 1 Vocabulary

1 Read and match the reviews with the movies.

> ~~an adventure movie~~   a comedy   a documentary   a drama   a musical
> a mystery   a science fiction movie   a superhero movie

1   It's about a family that goes around the world in a boat. Exciting and scary things happen to them along the way. It isn't a true story, but it feels real!
   <u>an adventure movie</u>

2   The year is 2080. All the people who live in the city are avatars! _____

3   Mrs. Brown's jewelry has disappeared. Everyone is trying to find out what happened to it. Every time you think you have the answer, you discover something new, and you don't know what to believe! _____

4   It's called *A Year in the Arctic*. You follow the daily life of an explorer there. I've learned amazing things about life in the Arctic. _____

5   It's really funny! I laughed so much; my stomach was hurting! _____

6   I love the songs and the dancing in this movie. The story is good, too.
   _____

7   It's about eight people who can do unusual things. For example, they can fly or live underwater! They help people in danger. _____

8   It's a story about a 15-year-old and what happens to him. It's sad, but it has a happy ending. _____

2 Choose three of your favorite kinds of movies from Activity 1. Write an example of each one.

Kind of movie	Title of movie
1 _____	_____
2 _____	_____
3 _____	_____

Student Book page 82

1 Read and complete. Use the correct form of the verbs.

Sandra
> I **want** to watch a comedy.

Alex
> *Sally and the Shoe Shop* **is** good. 😃

Marcus
> My favorite kind of movie **is** an adventure movie.

Corinne
> Some adventure movies **are** a bit scary.

Juan
> I **hate** scary movies. ☹️

Me
> I **don't know** what to do, because we all **like** different movies!

Sandra said she ¹ _____wanted_____ to watch a comedy. Alex said *Sally and the Shoe Shop* ² _____ good. Marcus said his favorite kind of movie ³ _____ an adventure movie. But Corinne said some adventure movies ⁴ _____ a bit scary. Juan said he ⁵ _____ scary movies. So I said I ⁶ _____ know what to do, because we ⁷ _____ _____ the same movies!

2 What did the people say? Write.

1 Jane: I love watching movies.

Jane said she loved watching movies.

2 Robert: I always close my eyes during scary movies.

_____

3 Peter and his friends: We want to watch a movie.

_____

4 My father: I don't go to the movie theater often.

_____

1 Read. Then complete the title of the interview. Use 1, 2, or 3.

1 Child Movie Star,   2 One of Hollywood's Top Movie Stars,   3 TV Star,

Two Minutes With

_____ Ashley Wilde

Have you seen *My Best Friend* yet? It's a very funny movie. It's hard to believe that 12-year-old Ashley Wilde hasn't been in a movie before. I'm sure we're going to see a lot of this young star on screen in the future!

I asked her how her movie work began. Ashley said she never thought about being a movie star, but she loved acting. She was in a school play when she met a famous movie director. He came to watch the play, because he wanted to find a new star for his next movie. He thought Ashley was an amazing actor. "And that was it!" said Ashley.

I asked her how she did her school work when she was making a film. Ashley said she had a tutor. She said child actors didn't have a lot of free time, because after filming, they had to do school work and study for exams.

I asked her what her friends thought about her success. She said her friends were very happy for her, but she was sad that she couldn't spend a lot of time with them now. She said, "I miss them, and the fun we always have together."

When I asked her what her future plans were, she said she wanted to make more movies and at the same time, she wanted do well at school. I asked her what she wanted to do first when she had some free time, and she said she wanted to go for a pizza with her friends!

2 Circle the correct answers.

1 *My Best Friend* is a **comedy** / **documentary**.

2 *My Best Friend* **is** / **isn't** the first movie that Ashley has acted in.

3 Ashley **always** / **didn't always** want to be a movie star.

4 When Ashley is filming, she **doesn't have to** / **also has to** do school work.

5 Ashley really wants to **be with her friends** / **do her school work** in her free time.

3 Write two questions the interviewer asked Ashley.

1 _How did your movie work begin?_ _____

2 _____

3 _____

Student Book page 84

1 Look at the Writing Tip. Write the correct punctuation.

1 "I enjoy being a movie star," Ashley said.

2 When do you do your school work I asked

3 I have a tutor said Ashley

> **Writing Tip!** To write the words that people say, use the correct punctuation.
>
> – Use quote marks.
>   *"Hello," she said.*
>
> – Use a comma before the last quote mark.
>   *"I love movies," said Mark.*
>
> – When it's a question, use a question mark instead of a comma before the last quote mark.
>   *"What's your favorite movie?" asked Ben.*

2 Write the report of your interview. Use the questions and answers in Activity 2 on page 85 of your Student Book. Remember to use the correct punctuation.

Two Minutes With _____

_____ is a movie star. Last week, I talked to _____

about _____ work.

I asked _____

_____

I asked _____

_____

I asked _____

_____

Lesson 5 Vocabulary

1 Unscramble the words.

1 cellexent   _excellent_

2 eningfright   _____

3 tingesinter   _____

4 sualunu   _____

5 prisinsurg   _____

6 illsy   _____

2 Complete the sentences. Use the words in Activity 1.

1 This movie is a comedy about someone who does ____silly____ things, for example, dancing around with a funny hat on.

2 It's an _____ movie! I loved everything about it. The actors were amazing, and the music was wonderful. It's the best movie I've ever seen!

3 The movie had a very _____ ending. I didn't think it was going to end that way. I still can't believe what happened in the end.

4 The movie was scary! I covered my eyes and ears in the most very _____ parts!

5 I watched an _____ documentary about life in the desert. I learned a lot of things about desert animals.

6 They made the whole movie underwater. It's a very difficult and _____ place to make a movie!

3 Write about three movies you've seen. Use words from Activity 1.

1 _____

2 _____

3 _____

Student Book page 86

1 Read and complete. Use reported speech.

Your work is excellent, Marina.

I don't have your homework yet, Lukas.

You can all watch a movie after lunch.

Alfie and Sofia, you can read your comics after school.

1   The teacher spoke to Marina. She told _____*her*_____ her work _____*was*_____ excellent.

2   The teacher spoke to Lukas. She told _____ she _____ _____ his homework yet.

3   The teacher spoke to me and the class. She told _____ we _____ all watch a movie after lunch.

4   The teacher spoke to Alfie and Sofia. She told _____ they _____ read their comics after school.

2 Rewrite the words in bold. Use pronouns and the correct form of the verbs.

1   Sally told **Tom, "You play** the guitar really well!"

Sally told him he played the guitar really well.

2   Anna told **the boy, "I want** to sing a silly song!"

_____

3   The teacher told **me and my friends, "You are** excellent students."

_____

4   I told **Mr. Bell, "I like** all your lessons!"

_____

5   Jack told **his friends, "I watched** a movie after school."

_____

Lesson 7 Arts

1 Complete the sentences.

> scene   sound   mood   lighting

1 My favorite _____ in the movie was when the children found their dog again.

2 When the light in a movie is bright and warm, the _____ is usually happy or exciting.

3 The movie director used clever _____ to make the street look dark and scary, even though it was in the day.

4 A very scary part of the mystery movie was the _____ of a door closing slowly.

2 Complete. Use the phrases below.

> a funny, silly, or happy mood   ~~bright lighting~~   cold colors and shadows   dark lighting
> exciting scenes   fast, loud music   frightening scenes   happy sounds   warm colors

1 Comedies and Musicals	2 Adventure or Mystery Movies	3 Scary Movies
bright lighting		

3 Think about a movie you've seen. Answer the questions.

1 What was the genre of the movie?

_____

2 What was the mood of the movie?

_____

3 What was your favorite scene?

_____

1 Look and complete the sentences. Use -y, -er, -less or -or.

1

He's an amazing act_o__r_!

2

Her arm is itch____.

3

Our math teach_____ is very clever.

4

My friend Helen is fear_____!

2 Complete the chart.

Word + Suffix =	New Word	Sentences
thirst + y =	1 _thirsty_	I need some water; I'm very __thirsty__.
farm + er =	2 _____	A _____ grows plants or has animals.
pain + less =	3 _____	It's OK; it's _____.
visit + or =	4 _____	You have a _____.

Progress Tracker

1 Complete the sentences. Use the words below.

> frightening   drama   documentary   silly   musical   science fiction
> surprising   superhero   interesting   ~~mystery~~

1   You don't know what's going to happen in a ___mystery___ movie.

2   _____ movies are about life in the future.

3   In funny movies, actors often do _____ things.

4   Some movies are very _____. I put my hands over my eyes!

5   The end of the movie was very _____. I thought the end might be different.

6   A _____ has a lot of songs and dancing in it.

7   *Super Kid* was the star of a _____ movie.

8   You can learn a lot of facts from a _____.

9   The movie wasn't boring at all. It was very _____.

10   My favorite movie is a _____ about a boy and his dog. It was sad.

2 Track it! Rate your progress in Unit 7.

I can name different kinds of movies. ☆ ☆ ☆ ☆ ☆

I can talk about what people said. ☆ ☆ ☆ ☆ ☆

I can read and understand a report of an interview. ☆ ☆ ☆ ☆ ☆

I can write a report of an interview. ☆ ☆ ☆ ☆ ☆

I can name more words to describe movies and books. ☆ ☆ ☆ ☆ ☆

I can make sentences with *told*. ☆ ☆ ☆ ☆ ☆

I can read and understand a text about movie genres. ☆ ☆ ☆ ☆ ☆

I can make a survey and talk about favorite movie genres. ☆ ☆ ☆ ☆ ☆

I can read and say words with the suffixes –*y*, –*er*, –*less*, and –*or*. ☆ ☆ ☆ ☆ ☆

Student Book page 91

Lesson 1 Vocabulary

1 Write the words in the crossword.

Across

3 pass ... exams

4 work ...

5 win an ...

7 get a ...

8 make a ...

Down

1 go to the ... party

2 go to a ... ceremony

6 ... a school sweatshirt

3 f i n a l

2 Complete. Use the phrases in Activity 1.

Lin: We're having an ¹ <u>end-of-year party</u>! Can you help me decorate the hall?

Toby: Of course! When will the party be?

Lin: I think we should have it after our ² _____ _____.

Toby: That's a good idea. Then our parents and teachers can come, too.

Lin: Who do you think will ³ _____ an _____ for the best results in the ⁴ _____ _____?

Toby: I think it will be you! You always ⁵ _____ _____ for the exams. But everyone will ⁶ _____ _____. I'll put mine on the wall!

Lin: Let's take pictures of each other at the party and ⁷ _____ _____.

Toby: Great idea! Let's ⁸ _____ _____ school _____ to wear!

Lesson 2 Grammar

1 Match the parts of the sentences.

1 If you work hard,

2 You'll win an award

3 If we have enough photos,

4 If I get a certificate,

5 I'll buy a school sweatshirt

6 If they have a graduation ceremony,

a my parents will go to it.

b I'll put it on the wall.

c we'll make a yearbook.

d if we have an end-of-year party.

e you'll pass your final exams.

f if you get the best marks in the final exams.

2 Complete the sentences. Use the correct form of the verbs in parentheses.

1 If we have an end-of-year party,
   I ___'ll choose___ the music. (choose)

2 I'll come to the party if it _____
   too late. (not end)

3 If I _____ my final exams, my
   parents will be very happy. (pass)

4 I _____ the party food with you
   if you want me to. (prepare)

5 You _____ more energy in the
   morning if you go to bed earlier. (have)

6 If you _____ things down, you'll remember them better. (write)

3 Complete the sentences for you. Use will.

1 If I work hard, I _____ .

2 If I have a party, I _____ .

3 If I get a certificate, my parents _____ .

1 Match the parts of the sentences.

Grade 6 Yearbook Jade

1 **My favorite day** — [d] — a was an actor who is in a new TV drama. We interviewed him, and he told us he was a student at our school once!

2 **Our class trip** — [ ] — b in the yearbook is the one of our whole class at the end-of-term party in April. We look very happy!

3 **My best class** — [ ] — c is don't forget your homework. If you forget your homework, Miss Henderson won't be happy!

4 **The most interesting person I met** — [ ] — d is Friday. We always watch movies in our English classes on Friday!

5 **My award** — [ ] — e was science. We made "snow," and it snowed all over Miss Henderson's table! That was fun!

6 **My happiest memory** — [ ] — f was the musical we wrote and performed at school for all the teachers, students, and parents. Everyone said it was excellent!

7 **My favorite picture** — [ ] — g for "The Silly Poem" competition was a surprise! I won first prize! 😄

8 **My advice to next year's Grade 6** — [ ] — h to the Natural History Museum was great! We learned a lot of interesting facts.

2 Read again. Then circle *True* or *False*.

1 The class watches movies in English class once a term. True / (False)

2 Jade was bored at the Natural History Museum. True / False

3 Something funny happened during Jade's science class. True / False

4 The class asked the actor some questions. True / False

5 Jade wrote a funny poem. True / False

6 The whole school performed in a musical. True / False

7 The class didn't have fun at the party in April. True / False

8 Miss Henderson will be happy if students forget their homework. True / False

Lesson 4 Writing

1 Look at the Writing Tip. Correct the punctuation.

1 ᴶjames is a student at ashton high school.

2 Its my friends favorite movie.

3 I worked hard and got a certificate, said suzy.

Writing Tip! Remember to check your work for punctuation.

– Use quote marks.
   "What's your favourite movie?"asked Ben.

– Use an apostrophe to show contractions and possession.
   It's Kevin's football.

– Use capital letters for names of people and for streets,
   towns, and places.
   Sally is having a birthday party. It's on King Street.

**2 Write your yearbook entry. Use the information in Activity 2 on page 95 of
your Student Book. Remember to check your work carefully.**

Student Book page 95

1 Find the words. Then complete the sentences.

b	o	r	e	d	e	r	i	q	e
c	p	a	p	e	r	c	n	w	a
l	b	r	a	v	e	l	t	o	d
o	t	w	o	o	l	a	e	r	s
n	v	g	n	l	d	y	r	r	f
e	w	o	o	d	d	u	e	i	g
l	l	a	s	t	i	c	s	e	h
y	p	r	o	u	d	a	t	d	j
p	l	e	a	s	e	d	e	w	k
k	i	o	e	u	s	c	d	b	m

1 My friends have all gone on vacation. I have nothing to do! I'm _____bored_____ and _____.

2 I'm _____ about this exam. Will I remember everything I have learned?

3 We're going to give Bethany her birthday gift. She'll be very _____!

4 I don't like spiders, but I'm going be _____ and hold it!

5 I got 100% in my final exam! Mom and Dad will be so _____ of me!

6 This book is amazing! I've always been _____ in the solar system.

2 How do you feel? Complete the sentences for you. Use the words in Activity 1.

How do you feel …

1 before an exam? _____

2 when you hear good news? _____

3 when you have nothing to do? _____

4 when you do well in something? _____

5 when your friends are on vacation? _____

6 when you watch an interesting TV show? _____

7 when you hold a spider in your hand (when you hate spiders!)? _____

1 **Write complete questions. Use *will*, *if*, and the correct form of the verbs in parentheses.**

1 What / you / do / you / (be) / bored / on the weekend?

What will you do if you're bored on the weekend?

2 Who / you / talk to / you / (be) / worried about something?

_____

3 What / you / wear / there / (be) / an end-of-year party?

_____

4 Who / you / call / you / (feel) / lonely?

_____

5 How / you / feel / you / (not pass) / your exams?

_____

6 What / we / get / we / (do) / well / in our final exams?

_____

2 **Complete the answers. Use the correct form of the verbs in parentheses.**

1 If I _____ feel _____ bored on the weekend, I _____ 'll play _____ a computer game. (feel, play)

2 If I _____ worried about something, I _____ to my mom. (feel, talk)

3 If there _____ an end-of-year party, I _____ a new T-shirt. (be, wear)

4 If I _____ lonely, I _____ you! (feel, call)

5 I _____ pleased if I _____ my exams. (not be, not pass)

6 We _____ a certificate if we _____ well in our final exams. (get, do)

3 **What will you do if you're bored on the weekend?**

_____

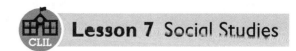

1 Complete. Use the words below.

> achievement   age   college   ~~decided~~
> degree   succeed

James: Have you ¹ _decided_ what you're going to do when you finish high school?

Cathy: Yes, I have! I want to go to ² _____ and get a ³ _____ in music. Then I want to become a famous musician.

James: That's a great idea! I've heard you playing the piano. You're amazing! When did you start playing the piano?

Cathy: When I was six years old. And when I was eight, I won an award in an international music competition.

James: Really? That's a great ⁴ _____ for your ⁵ _____ ! If you continue to work hard and practice a lot, I'm sure you'll ⁶ _____ and become a famous musician! Your parents will be very proud of you.

2 Read the text on page 98 of your Student Book again. Circle the correct answers.

1 When he was young, Kieron Williamson was interested …

   a in many things, including art.   b only in art.

2 He … six pictures a week.

   a sold   b painted

3 Kieron has … a lot of other famous artists.

   a taught   b learned from

4 Nola Ochs went to college because she …

   a wanted to inspire young people.   b enjoyed learning.

5 She got a college degree …

   a when she was 96.   b in 1911.

1 Complete the sentences. Use contractions.

| 're | 'm | 've | 's | 'll | 't |

1

He can't talk yet. (he can not)

2

_____ passed my final exam! (I have)

3

_____ a ten-year-old boy. (I am)

4

_____ a smart girl. (she is)

5

_____ from Australia. (they are)

6

_____ won the football match! (we will)

2 Complete the chart.

Word + Word =	New Word	Sentences
can + not =	1 ____can't____	No, you ____can't____ go out now.
I + am =	2 _____	_____ tired now.
he + is =	3 _____	_____ my best friend.
they + are =	4 _____	_____ very funny!
she + will =	5 _____	_____ help you.
you + have =	6 _____	_____ done well!

Student Book page 100

1 Complete the sentences. Use the words below.

> certificate   passed   ~~worried~~   hard   yearbook   brave   bored
> lonely   pleased and proud   end-of-year

1 I feel _____worried_____ when I think something bad is going to happen.

2 I feel _____ when I do well in my exams.

3 If you work _____, you'll do well and get a _____.

4 I want to go to the _____ party.

5 At the end of the year, it's fun to make a _____.

6 We've _____ our final exams!

7 A firefighter has to be _____.

8 If you have friends, you won't feel _____.

9 If you have a lot of hobbies, you won't feel _____.

2 Track it! Rate your progress in Unit 8.

I can name end-of-year activities. ☆☆☆☆☆

I can make predictions in the future with *if* and *will*. ☆☆☆☆☆

I can read and understand a yearbook entry. ☆☆☆☆☆

I can write a yearbook entry. ☆☆☆☆☆

I can name words to describe how people feel. ☆☆☆☆☆

I can ask and answer questions with *Wh–* words and *if.* ☆☆☆☆☆

I can read and understand a text about people's achievements. ☆☆☆☆☆

I can make a certificate and talk about achievements. ☆☆☆☆☆

I can read and say words with contractions. ☆☆☆☆☆

1 Check (✔) all the facts that the biography tells us about Hokusai.

1 He came from Japan.

2 From a young age, he wanted to be an artist.

3 His father wasn't an artist.

4 A famous artist called Katsukawa was one of Hokusai's teachers.

5 Hokusai worked in a bookstore for many years.

6 He was the first artist to paint Mount Fuji.

7 He painted *The Great Wave* when he was 75.

2 Match the parts of the sentences.

1 When Hokusai was 12,　　　　　　　　a when he was an old man.

2 His first pictures　　　　　　　　　　b he painted *The Great Wave*.

3 In his books, there were　　　　　　　c he worked in a bookstore.

4 His most famous pictures　　　　　　d were pictures of Mount Fuji.

5 He painted Mount Fuji　　　　　　　e pictures of plants, animals, and people.

6 When he was 75,　　　　　　　　　　f were pictures of famous actors
　　　　　　　　　　　　　　　　　　　　from musicals.

3 Answer the questions.

1 What are three adjectives or phrases to describe Hokusai before the shogun invited him to a competition?

_____

2 What did Hokusai use to make his painting of leaves on a river?

_____

3 What four ways did Hokusai want to paint Mount Fuji?

_____

4 Much later, Hokusai's paintings inspired two famous artists. Who were they?

_____

4 Think. Answer the questions.

1 Would you like to be a famous painter one day? Why or why not?

_____

_____

2 Do you like Hokusai's paintings? Why or why not?

_____

_____

3 Why are biographies important? What can we learn from them?

_____

_____

1 Look and circle.

b	a	n	g	s	a	r	i	q	s
c	u	r	l	y	r	c	n	w	t
l	m	r	a	v	e	l	t	o	r
o	u	w	o	o	l	a	e	r	a
b	s	g	n	b	e	a	r	d	i
a	t	o	o	d	q	u	w	i	g
l	a	a	s	t	i	c	a	e	h
d	c	r	o	u	d	a	v	d	t
s	h	e	a	s	e	d	y	e	k
k	e	e	y	e	b	r	o	w	s

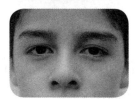

2 Complete.

We made a snow woman! She's wearing a black and white

1 ___scarf___ and a long 2 _____ around her

neck. She's wearing a 3 _____, and she's carrying

a 4 _____!

We made a snow man, too! He's wearing a 5 _____

around his neck and 6 _____ on his hands. He has a

7 _____ around his middle, and he's wearing a pair

of 8 _____!

1 Look and complete.

Is your dog
1 f r i e n d l y ?

Yes, he is! He's very
2 a_____ l_____ _____ c and he's
3 s_____ _____ t, too. He can do
4 f_____ n_____ tricks.

I'm not nervous.
I'm the opposite! I feel very
6 c_____ f_____ d_____.

5 Q_____ _____ t, please!

Thank you! You are all very
7 p_____ t_____ _____ t! And you are very
8 k_____ _____ to help me.

2 Write the adverbs.

1 quiet ___quietly___   2 slow _____

3 patient _____   4 loud _____

5 good _____   6 quick _____

7 careful _____   8 bad _____

3 Write the opposites.

1 quietly _____   2 slowly _____   3 well _____

1 Complete the words and match to the pictures.

1 b _a_ _k_ _e_ _r_ _y_

3 police s____ t____ n

5 m____ e____

7 t____ a____ r

2 b____ k

4 f____ e st____ ____ ____ n

6 s____ d____ m

8 p____ t o____ i____

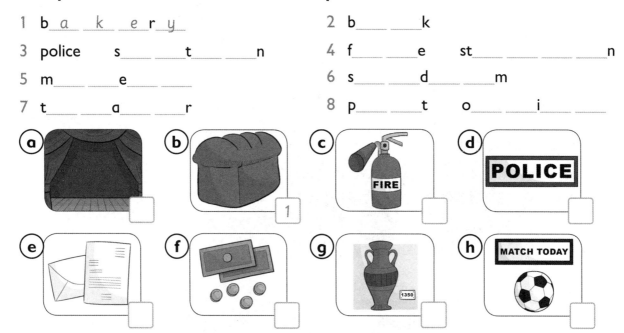

a

b [1]

c FIRE

d POLICE

e

f

g 1350

h MATCH TODAY

2 Look and complete.

along   between   don't   left (x2)   over   past   ~~right~~   straight   turn

Hi, Dan! I'm here in front of the train station. The bakery is across from me. How do I get to the museum?

Hi, Amy! Turn 1 _____right_____, and walk to the end of the street. 2 _____ turn left into Park Road; go 3 _____. At the corner, there's a river. Go 4 _____ the bridge, and then turn 5 _____. Walk 6 _____ the river. Go 7 _____ the school and the post office. Then 8 _____ right. This is Birch Road. The museum is on the 9 _____, 10 _____ the bank and the police station.

Ash Road

Bank

Museum

Police Station

Birch Road

Post Office

West Road

Tree Road

Park Road

Train Station

River Are

School

1 Complete the crossword.

Across

(1) (4) (5) (7) (8)

Down

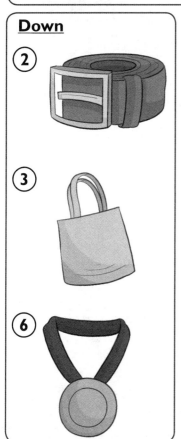

(2) (3) (6)

1 p	2 l	a	s	t	i	3 c

4

5 6

7

8

2 Unscramble the words.

1 Sugar is sweet, but lemons are (rosu) _____sour_____.

2 Pablo thinks spinach is (robhiler) _____, but I love it! I think it's (sciouilde) _____.

3 It isn't cheap. It's (visenexep) _____.

4 Ice cream isn't (darh) _____ like candy. Ice cream is (tofs) _____.

Word Work Unit 5

1 Match.

1 explore   a famous person

2 sleep in   a snake

3 ride   a volcano

4 see   a hot air balloon

5 go on   a camel

6 hold   a rainforest

7 fly in   the desert

8 climb   the pyramids

9 meet   a safari

2 Complete the sentences.

1 A k _a_ _n_ g_____ _____ _____o lives in Australia. It can jump very high.

2 A p_____ l_____ b_____ _____r lives on the ice in the Arctic.

3 A s_____ w l_____ p_____ _____d lives in the mountains in Asia.

4 A s_____ t_____ moves very slowly and sleeps a lot.

5 The o_____ _____r_____ _____h is the biggest bird on the planet. It can run very fast, but it can't fly.

6 A m_____ _____s_____ is a big animal. It lives in the forest and can swim very well.

7 A j_____g_____ _____r is a big cat from South America.

8 An e_____g_____ _____ is a big bird that can fly very well.

1 Look and write.

1 make a c o s t u m e

2 send an

    _____

3 _____ the
   party food

4 _____ the music

5 _____
   the yard

6 _____
   the games

7 buy the _____

8 _____ chairs

o	z	c	d	i	o	b	e	z	k	c
r	x	o	f	k	t	o	t	o	w	j
g	p	s	w	l	y	r	h	r	q	i
a	l	t	h	r	p	r	i	z	e	s
n	h	u	w	q	g	o	e	o	d	c
i	k	m	r	o	i	w	t	w	g	h
z	j	e	y	e	w	l	i	h	m	o
e	p	r	e	p	a	r	e	k	n	o
d	e	c	o	r	a	t	e	f	o	s
i	n	v	i	t	a	t	i	o	n	e

2 Unscramble the words.

Let's all [1] (rowk gotthree) _____work_____ ____together____ to help our

neighbors in our [2] (higherboonod) _____!

• Collect the [3] (lami) _____

• [4] (Trawe) _____ the plants

• Be a [5] (rotut) _____

• Be a [6] (lotuvener) _____

• Put litter in a [7] (shart nac) _____ _____

1 Complete the sentences.

1 *Journey to the Future* is a s c i e n c e f i c t i o n movie.

2 *The Life of a Dolphin* is a great d_____ _____ _____ _____ _____ _____ _____ y.

3 *The Lost Jewels* is a m_____ _____ _____ _____ y movie with a surprising end.

4 *Catgirl and Catboy to the Rescue!* is an exciting s_____ _____ _____ _____ _____ _____ o movie.

5 *Don't be Silly, Sid!* is a very funny c_____ _____ _____ y.

6 *Music and Dance* is a good m_____ _____ _____ _____ l.

7 *The Island* is an exciting a_____ _____ _____ _____ _____ _____ e movie.

8 *Friends Forever* is my favorite d_____ _____ a.

2 Unscramble the words.

1 My favorite movie is about a man called Mr. Fish. He does very (lysil) _____silly_____ things!

2 I can't watch scary movies. They're too (ginfenright) _____.

3 I watch a lot of documentaries about history. They're always (eterinsting) _____.

4 It's a very (sunaulu) _____ movie. There's no music in it, and nobody speaks!

5 I thought that movie was (tenlexcel) _____!

6 It's a mystery movie, and it has a lot of (prisrusing) _____ events.

Student Book pages 82 and 86

1 Unscramble the words.

1 Go to a (ationugrad onmycere) <u>graduation ceremony</u> and get a

(cercatetifi) _____ .

2 Win an (waard) _____ .

3 Work (arhd) _____ and pass your (nialf) _____ exams.

4 Buy a school (stweashirt) _____ to wear at the end-of-year

(ptyar) _____ .

5 Make a (boyeaokr) _____ .

2 Complete the sentences. Use the words below.

| bored | brave | interested | lonely | pleased | proud | ~~worried~~ |

1 I've worked hard, so I'm not ____<u>worried</u>____ about my final exams. I think I'll do well!

2 Mom will be very _____ that I've tidied my room!

3 Jessica's very _____ in animals. She loves documentaries about them.

4 I'm _____! Let's play a game!

5 It's difficult to start a new school when you don't know anyone. But be _____!

You'll soon make new friends, and then you won't feel _____ .

6 My parents will be very _____ of me when I get my certificate.

Macmillan Education Limited
4 Crinan Street
London N1 9XW

Companies and representatives throughout the world

Share It! Level 6 Workbook ISBN 978-1-380-02324-7

Share It! Level 6 Workbook and Digital Workbook
ISBN 978-1-380-06948-1

Text, design and illustration Macmillan Education Limited 2020
Written by Cheryl Pelteret

Original design by Pronk Media, Inc.

Page make-up by SPi Technologies, Inc.

Illustrated by Alla Badsar (Advocate Art) pp. 9; Tom Heard (Bright Agency) pp. 88, 89, 90, 91; Dave Williams (Bright Agency) pp. 4, 6, 7, 8, 10, 17, 18, 19, 21, 22, 24, 29, 30, 32, 33, 34, 35, 37, 38, 39, 41, 42, 44, 48, 49, 50, 57, 63, 68, 72, 74, 81, 83.

Cover design by Roberto Martinez, Marcin Rojek, and Wojciech Szulik

Cover illustration Emi Ordás

Cover photograph by Getty Images/iStock/Pollyana Ventura, Getty Images/Hero Images

Picture research by Sarah Wells

The authors and publishers would like to thank the following for permission to reproduce their photographs:

123RF/Lightfieldstudios p8(8);

Alamy Stock Photo/Classic Image p14, Alamy Stock Photo/Cultura RM p8(1);

Comstock p75(2);

Alamy Stock Photo/Aleksandr Belugin p. 84(1.3), Alamy Stock Photo/FLPA p. 52(5), Alamy Stock Photo/Konstantin Pelikh p. 84(1.6), Alamy Stock Photo/PHOTOINKE p. 84(1.5);

BananaStock/Punchstock p.88(7);

Getty Images/Bettmann p. 23, Getty Images/Caiaimage/Martin Barraud p. 75(1.3), Getty Images/Corbis NX/Richard Leo Johnson p. 35(1.1), Getty Images/Corbis/Fuse p. 52(2), Getty Images/Cultura RF/Steve Sparrow p. 15(a), Getty Images/DigitalVision/Ariel Skelley p. 28(t), Getty Images/DigitalVision/Jose Luis Pelaez Inc p. 55(1), Getty Images/DigitalVision/Leren Lu p. 92(t), Getty Images/E+/dageldog p. 24(1.2), Getty Images/E+/dzphotovideo p. 75(1.4), Getty Images/E+/Flavio Vallenari p. 47, Getty Images/E+/skodonnell p. 55(4), Getty Images/EyeEm/David Garcia p.88(8), Getty Images/EyeEm/Kukiat Boontung p. 12(4), Getty Images/EyeEm/Pongsak Tawansaeng p. 75(1.2), Getty Images/EyeEm/Rene Becerril pp. 52(3), 92(b), Getty Images/EyeEm/Visut Thepkunhanimit p. 64(1.3), Getty Images/Gallo Images/David Malan p. 15(b), Getty Images/Glow Images p. 28(b), Getty Images/Hero Images p.88(6), Getty Images/iStock/clu p. 12(2), Getty Images/iStock/Goldfinch4ever p. 64(1.4), Getty Images/iStock/heinteh p. 12(6, down), Getty Images/iStock/Jiradelta p. 12(6, up), Getty Images/iStock/NYS444 p. 12(5), Getty Images/iStock/paleka19 p. 12(1), Getty Images/iStock/quintanilla p. 55(3), Getty Images/iStock/redhumv p. 14, Getty Images/iStock/Vladimiroquai p. 24(1.4), Getty Images/iStockphoto/Thinkstock Images/bloodua p. 54(pineapple), Getty Images/iStockphoto/Thinkstock Images/Jan Will p. 52(1), Getty Images/JGI/Jamie Grill pp. 15(c), 84(1.2) Getty Images/Moment Open/Will Guthrie p.88(5), Getty Images/SSC/Stone p.88(2), Getty Images/Stockbyte pp. 10(I), 88(4), Getty Images/Stockbyte/SW Productions p. 84(1.1), Getty Images/Stockbyte/Tom Brakefield pp. 52(6), 52(4), Getty Images/Stone/Coneyl Jay p. 94, Getty Images/The Image Bank/Nivek Neslo p. 77, Getty Images/Thinkstock Images/Photodisc p.88(1), Getty Images/Thinkstock/Stockbyte p. 95;

ImageSource p. 88(3), ImageSource/Steve Prezant p. 84(1.4);

Kevin McCabe pp. 43, 46(b);

Photodisc p. 54(coconut);

Royalty_free/Corbis p. 46(t);

Shutterstock/Andrey_Popov p. 24(1.1), Shutterstock/Artem Avetisyan p. 12(7), Shutterstock/AZLAN LOW p. 64(1.1), Shutterstock/bonvoyagecaptain p. 35(1.3), Shutterstock/Carboxylase p. 10(emoji's), Shutterstock/Evgeny Ternovetsky p. 15(d), Shutterstock/Hennadii H p. 64(1.2), Shutterstock/Jonas Petrovas p. 75(1.1), Shutterstock/Myvisuals p. 12(3), Shutterstock/Sergei25 p. 52(7), Shutterstock/Yiorgos GR p. 55(2);

Macmillan Education Ltd. /David Tolley p. 54(mango).

Printed and bound in Poland by CGS

2025 2024 2023 2022 2021

21 20 19 18 17 16 15 14 13 12